In this series –

RUMI READINGS
FOR
MINDFULNESS

RUMI READINGS
FOR
MINDFULNESS

JALALUDDIN RUMI

The Scholengrade Foundation

The Scheherazade Foundation CIC
85 Great Portland Street
London
W1W 7LT
United Kingdom
www.SF.Charity
info@SF.Charity

First published by The Scheherazade Foundation CIC, 2025

RUMI READINGS FOR MINDFULNESS

© The Scheherazade Foundation

The Scheherazade Foundation asserts the right to be identified as the Author
of the Work in accordance with the Copyright, Designs and Patents Act 1988.

A CIP catalogue record for this title is available from the British Library.

ISBN 978-1-915311-76-4

Introduction

Jalaluddin Rumi was born in Balkh, Afghanistan, in the year 1207, and died in Konya, Turkey, in 1273.

During the sixty-six years spanning this pair of dates, he produced a range of extraordinary work in Persian which, today, is classed as 'Sufi Mysticism'.

In the seven and a half centuries since his death, Rumi's corpus, which includes *The Masnavi* and *Fihi Ma Fihi*, has been circulated widely across the Near East, the Arab world, and Central Asia.

Generations of students continue to commit selections of the 60,000 verses to heart, and allow Rumi's way of thought to permeate through all areas of their lives.

Although Orientalists venturing eastward from Europe in the 1700s occasionally made note of Sufi Mysticism, they tended to witness it through the more theatrical frills – such as 'whirling dervishes' – rather than through a deep appreciation of the texts.

It wasn't until the close of the nineteenth century that the first wholescale translations of Rumi's written work began to appear in Europe.

Even then, they remained very much the purview of a few academics, whose translations were – even for the time – laden with indescribably floral and cumbersome prose.

Although in the Occident, students would find themselves scrutinizing Rumi's corpus, it wasn't until more recently that accessible appreciations of his work became available.

A few years before his death, I asked my father – the Sufi scholar and thinker Idries Shah – for his thoughts on Rumi's legacy in the West.

Sitting in his favourite chair, a porcelain cup of green tea in hand, he looked at me hard.

'I never cease to be amazed,' he said.

'Amazed by what?'

'By the way people don't take what's perfectly packaged, and ready and waiting for them, but rather obsess with something else.'

'With what?'

'With endless and nonsensical trimmings, trappings, and paraphernalia.'

My father sipped his tea.

After a moment of silent thought, he continued:

'Read Rumi in the original Persian,' he said, 'and so delicate are the verses that you have tears rolling down your cheeks. Yet here in the West, it's served up as something submerged in a thick, glutinous gravy, so much so that its utterly inedible.'

I reminded my father that a series of publications had recently found their way to press – publications that presented Rumi's couplets in an utterly new way.

Stripped bare of what my father had referred to as 'gravy', they were light.

Indeed, they were lighter than light.

My father rolled his eyes at the thought.

'In any other place, and at any other time,' he said, 'people would be up in arms. Or, if they weren't, they'd be laughing until their sides split. Imagine it – Western poets with absolutely no knowledge of the original Persian text touting new, bestselling editions of Rumi's work! It's what we call "The Soup of the Soup of the Soup".'

In the years since my father's death, Occidental society has been flooded with all things Rumi.

Couplets ascribed to him are read solemnly at weddings across the United States, Europe, and beyond.

Wisdom drawn from his poetry is tattooed daily over the backs and limbs of Hollywood A-listers.

But the precious words uttered at weddings, tattooed into skin, and quoted in abundance, hold little or no bearing to the original verses of Jalaluddin Rumi.

So, there it is…

The great Sufi Master's wisdom available:

(a) in a form that's unreadable because it's all covered in glutinous gravy, or

(b) in another form that's completely distorted – the Soup of the Soup of the Soup.

One thing that *is* evident is that the West can benefit enormously from a clean, clear rendition of Rumi's thinking – as the East has done over the last seven hundred years.

For this reason, we have commissioned entirely new translations, gleaned in particular from *The Masnavi*. Selected and translated by native Persian-speaking scholars, the emphasis has been on maintaining the lightness of Rumi's poetry.

In an age of relentless speed and digital overload, and so as to allow the work to be accessed by those who may benefit from it most, we have arranged a series of bite-sized morsels by way of theme.

We encourage you to do what students, scholars, and ordinary people have done across the East for centuries...

To pick a single couplet, or a handful – and to read them over and over, allowing them to seed themselves in your mind.

Little by little, having taken root, they will blossom and bear fruit.

Tahir Shah

How to Use This Book

Rumi Readings for Mindfulness

This book is not in a hurry.

It is not here to overwhelm, instruct, or impress.

It is here to help you come back to the moment you are already in.

Rumi Readings for Mindfulness gathers one hundred quotes drawn from *The Masnavi* and other works by the Sufi master, translated freshly from the original Persian by The Scheherazade Foundation. These are not fragments of inspiration. They are invitations – to notice more closely, to soften inwardly, to wake up to life with a gentler kind of attention.

Mindfulness, in Rumi's world, is not a trend.

It is not about performance or perfection.

It is a return – to the breath, to awareness, to the divine pulse within and around us.

These quotes are divided into ten themes that move through different forms of attention: noticing the self, observing thought, practising restraint, recognizing illusion, engaging in presence, and remembering what is real.

They are not rules.
They are reminders.

Let them enter your day like light through a small window.

A Quiet Companion

You do not need to read this book all at once.
You don't even need to read a full page. One line may be enough.

Begin your day by opening the book at random. Or read it before sleep. Let a single quote be your companion for the day.

Let it interrupt your auto-pilot. Let it reorient your gaze.

Mindfulness doesn't always arrive in meditation. Sometimes it begins with noticing the way you hold your coffee, the sound in someone's voice, or the breath you forgot you were holding.

Let these words be small wake-up calls.
Not jarring. Just honest.

No Need to Understand It All

Rumi's language, even in translation, is layered.
You may not 'get it' on the first reading. That's okay.

Mindfulness invites us to experience things as they are –
not as we wish they were.
Approach these quotes the same way.

Don't force clarity. Let it come, or not.

Some lines may return to you later, unannounced. That's
their way of working.

Reflect, If You Wish

If a quote resonates – or confuses you – you might write
about it. Sit with it. Ask yourself:

- What is this making me notice?
- Where do I see this in my life?

- What part of me is reacting to this?

You don't need to come to answers.

It's not another task. It's a tool for presence.

Carry It Into Your Day

You might find a quote that stays with you – in your breath, in your work, in the way you speak to someone. That's the point.

Mindfulness isn't a pause from life. It's life lived differently.

Let a line walk beside you during your commute. Let it soften you at the moment you're about to react. Let it remind you to look up.

Share With Intention

Some quotes may resonate so clearly that you want to share them. With a friend. A student. A group. Go ahead.

These lines were made to move – not only within us, but between us.

You might find a quote says something you've been trying to express for a long time. Let it speak for you.

This Is a Practice

You may not feel mindful today. Or tomorrow. You may forget the quote. You may forget to open the book. That's okay.

This book will not shame you for being human.

Rumi meets us where we are – distracted, striving, unsure – and gently reminds us to return.

He writes in this volume:
'Exercise self-control and refrain from wandering thoughts. For thoughts are like fierce lions, and hearts like untamed jungles. Self-control is the key... Hold these words of mine close, as you might decorate your ears with earrings, and I will transform you into something valuable, like a golden earring itself.'

Let that transformation be slow.

Let it be quiet.

Let it be yours.

Part 1
Factors Influencing the Growth of Awareness

1

O you who have become lost in laziness
and unable to distinguish others from yourself,
'essence' refers to something that exists independently,
while 'accident' refers to something
that is subordinate and less important.

2

Once the fruit reaches maturity and develops sweetness,
it gently bites its own lips
and releases its hold on the branch.

3

A wise person understands fundamental meaning;
they do not prioritize quantity
as it has become less important.

4

Division emerges as a result of polytheistic belief
and the concept of duality,
while unity is inherent within the spiritual essence.

5

Patience is more incisive than a steel blade,
and more triumphant than a hundred armies.

6

Mary sought refuge by the blessed tree
once she began to suffer the pains of labour:
the onset of childbirth drove her to the trunk of a palm,
compelling her to seek solace there,
and the withered tree yielded fruit.
The human body might be compared to Mary,
each person possessing their own personal Jesus.
When we feel pain, it signifies the birth of our own Jesus.
But in the absence of grief,
Jesus will retreat to the hidden path
from which he originated,
leaving us bereft and devoid of advantage.

7

Exercise self-control
and refrain from wandering thoughts.
For thoughts are like fierce lions,
and hearts like untamed jungles.
Self-control is the key,
as scratching merely makes the irritation worse.
Hold these words of mine close,
as you might decorate your ears with earrings,
and I will transform you into something valuable,
like a golden earring itself.

8

Within this fertile ground,
within this untainted expanse,
let us cultivate only the seeds of affection.

9

Your dissatisfaction stems solely
from your longing for what you desire;
otherwise, all your desires would be fulfilled effortlessly,
like gifts.

10

It is better to die from lack of resources
than to be dependent on others, like a parrot.
Embrace self-sufficiency,
and accept your own state of need and poverty.

Part 2
Barriers to Growth & Awareness

11

Water can extinguish external fires,
but the fire of desire leads to hell.

12

It is unwise and futile to search for your identity
among the chaos of 'self' and 'mine',
as this sorrow serves as a diversion from true essence.

13

People with a materialistic mind
have a debased and indulgent nature.
As a result, their rationality is undermined,
and their aspirations inevitably lead
to their own downfall.

14

Exercise prudence with your desires and wishes,
as they can divert you from the righteous path of God.

15

Divinity is the mantle of the Majestic One;
anyone who dons it will be encumbered by its weight.
The crown belongs to Him alone,
and those who excessively boast about their own
might will inevitably find destruction.

16

Unless a person experiences annihilation of the Self,
they cannot enter the Court of Majesty.

17

Genuine alchemy is the process of transforming
and rejuvenating suffering;
it is not found in situations
where comfort is derived solely from the absence of pain.
Do not express sorrow with a sigh;
actively pursue the source of suffering,
and continue to do so.

18

Satan is intrinsically opposed to human souls;
his satisfaction comes from the destruction of humanity.
His inherent malevolence, though unfounded,
drives him towards tyranny and evil.

19

The cunning of devils
gives them knowledge of our
private thoughts and convictions,
enabling them to use their techniques
to steal our inner essence.
Their acts of theft have led to our downfall.

20

The lamp of guidance has spoken truth:
both this world and the hereafter are harmful.
Being attached to this world
means being disconnected from the hereafter,
and the comfort of the physical body
can be detrimental to the well-being of the soul.

Part 3
Stages of Awareness

21

In the beginning,
he entered the domain of lifeless entities,
and subsequently transitioned
from lifelessness to the realm of plants.
He spent years in a vegetative state,
completely unaware of his prior existence
as an inanimate being.

22

It is strange, O honourable one,
that you do not seek refuge in the realm
of absolute certainty.
Each doubt yearns for assurance, child,
yet futilely flutters its wings, unable to ascend.

23

Once a person attains knowledge,
their wings and feet gain stability
and their knowledge ignites and energizes certainty.
Along the journey, knowledge is inferior to certainty,
but superior to mere suspicion.

24

This limited intelligence originates
from the Universal Intellect,
and the motion of this silhouette stems
from the branch of that flower.
The omniscient Creator guides the being's progression
from its animal state toward human form.

25

Understand that knowledge inherently pursues certainty,
and certainty, in turn, pursues a clear
and insightful understanding.
Search for this phrase in the book *Al-Hakim*[1] immediately
following the statement:
'Indeed, if only you knew.'

---

1   A classic book on magic.

26

The soul is liberated from
the physical attributes of the body,
but a body devoid of a soul is lifeless and without value.
Explore beyond the animal soul
and delve into the human soul.

27

Transcend the limitations of human existence
and the clamour of debate
until you reach the boundary
of Gabriel's vast expanse of the inner Self.
Even Ahmad's[2] spirit suppresses its emotions
while Gabriel retreats in terror.

---

2 Another name for the Prophet Muhammad.

28

Acquiring knowledge leads to the ability to perceive
and understand things clearly.
By achieving lucidity,
you will be able to perceive hell with total clarity.
Vision arises from unwavering certainty,
without hesitation,
while imagination comes from uncertainty.

29

On experiencing the delightful flavour of His divine grace,
my perception was heightened and illuminated
by His profound insight.

30

I received both the message of Truth and its greeting
from someone of refined sensibility.
This salutation, which brings me more joy than any scent,
encapsulates the very essence of everything I cherish.

Part 4

The Role of Language in Human Development

31

Hold your peace,
as verbal communication highlights division;
otherwise, like a young boy eating bread,
there would be no necessity to converse while eating.

32

Remain silent,
like the dead,
O heart,
as we are being charged with the act of being alive
by this very tongue.

33

Do not speak,
for the tongue is all harm.
Why do you run towards harm?

34

Stop, as verbal expression serves as a barrier
that conceals your true thoughts and emotions.
I wish for my heart be ignorant of this language.

35

See beyond definitions and focus on attributes,
allowing them to direct you towards the essence.
Variations among individuals stem from their names;
but when they delve further into meaning,
peace is discovered.

36

As a result of their disagreements,
certain people have become entangled in disputes,
completely unaware of the meaning of names.

37

Language serves as a conduit for meaning,
but how can a vast sea of ideas and concepts
be effectively expressed
through such a narrow channel?

38

Subject the defiant structure to anguish
in order to reveal the underlying harmony,
like a valuable jewel.
If you fail to dissolve it,
His benefits will dissolve on their own.
O my heart,
He is the divine ruler.

39

When the heart is in a state of bliss,
words spoken by the tongue can be destructive,
and thoughts, like al-Araf,[3]
serve as a breeding ground for sin and wrongdoing.

---

3   The realm between heaven and hell.

40

Music serves as nourishment for lovers,
stimulating their idea of union.

Part 5

Methods for Gaining Awareness

41

Discover the interpretation of the Qur'an
by referring to the Qur'an itself
and seeking guidance from those
who have transcended worldly ambition.
Before engaging with the Qur'an,
it is necessary to cultivate
a state of humility and self-restraint,
so that your innermost being reflects
its teachings and principles.

42

Rational thought, much like the angel Gabriel,
can offer guidance,
but if it leads you astray, it can cause harm.
As the sovereign of your soul,
you must recognize when to stop letting it direct you,
as its scope is limited.

43

The heart is a reservoir of illumination.
Can it be the dwelling of God yet lack vision?
No, the heart encompasses many specific
and broad characteristics.
But which one is the true essence?

44

The writings of the Sufi are more than mere words;
no heart is as pure as snow.
The scholar gains wisdom from written texts.
But what does the Sufi possess?
The traces of their journey.

45

Love is a subject beyond debate,
and surpasses all other matters.
It transforms conversation into a fervent plea for help.
The profound awe that love inspires
transcends verbal expression.
No one can fully grasp the depth of this experience.

46

In the realm of love
you may discover profound truths
that transcend conventional reasoning,
marked by their magnificence and meaning.
This surpasses the intellectual capacity
that governs the operations of celestial bodies.
Your knowledge enables you to provide nourishment
and organize the heavenly realms.

47

Embrace foolishness and follow the path of the fool,
and you will find salvation within this folly.
The Prophet of humanity has said
that the majority of the inhabitants of Paradise are
those who lack worldly wisdom.
To maintain a pure heart, it is advisable
to choose foolishness as a means to counteract
the presence of pride and arrogance,
which are constant companions.

48

Upon my demise as a mortal being,
my faculties of hearing, perception, and sight
were replaced by Truth.
In this intense state of euphoria
I no longer identify with my usual Self.
Therefore, anyone who maintains their sense of Self
during this moment
can be considered an unbeliever.

49

Detoxify your being from inherent qualities
to perceive the untainted core of your own identity.
The knowledge of the Prophets can be found
within your heart, independent of books, temples,
or scriptures like the Avesta.[4]

---

4   The book of Zoroastrian religious texts.

50

When a profound and heartfelt cry emerges,
it initiates the process of forgiveness,
much like the stirring of a vast ocean.
Amidst the weeping, in a dream,
a vivid image of an elderly man materializes.

Part 6

Indicators of the Growth
of Spiritual Intelligence

51

Once you have fully comprehended
and internalized profound truths,
you will attain reason,
freeing yourself from mere imitation
and experiencing liberation of the heart.

52

A town can make ten men foolish,
diminishing their intelligence
and draining them of brightness and vitality.
The villagers' understanding remains incomplete
until the day comes to an end.
A village is essentially a place
where an elderly person, having achieved nothing,
engages in imitation and futile debates.

53

Strive to find a valuable treasure
that makes the concept of gaining
or losing less important.
Devote yourself to this pursuit,
regarding everything else as insignificant side effects.
Those who plant wheat seeds
will inevitably obtain straw.

54

Knowledge is the foundation of Solomon's kingdom,
encompassing all aspects of creation,
both physical and spiritual.
When humanity attains this,
it surpasses even the creation of oceans,
mountains, and plains.

55

Associate with people
who hold profound meaning
to gain both blessings and cultivate good character.

56

According to the Prophet,
Paradise is a divine gift.
If you desire it,
do not ask for anything from others.
If you do not ask,
I will guarantee your access to Paradise
and the divine sight of God.

57

Through a gradual process of spiritual
detachment and self-annihilation,
you progress toward the ultimate goal of union with God.

58

These pillars represent the imperfections of the world,
while also serving as cures for hidden ailments.
Motivated solely by love and compassion,
they act without ulterior motives or incentives,
much like the Divine.
Why do you offer assistance in a solitary occurrence?
They reply:
'To express sadness and a sense of helplessness.'

59

I discovered the secret by seeking knowledge
from the ultimate reality.
As a result, the most direct and correct path
was revealed to me.
He explained that the purpose of this coin,
though modest in size, was to express a child's distress.
Compassion floods the heart
only when the child selling halva sheds tears.

60

A pilgrim seeks a fellow traveller to accompany them
on their sacred journey,
regardless of religious or cultural background,
whether Hindu, Turk, or Arab.
Disregard physical appearance or colour;
instead, focus on determination and purpose.
If someone has different skin colour
but aligns with your objective,
acknowledge them as your peer,
for they share the same fundamental qualities as you.

Part 7

Alterations in Personality Along the Path of Growth & Development

61

It was said:
'You are not insane;
you are simply not suited for this place.'
I left, succumbed to madness,
and confined myself with chains.

62

It was said:
'You are not drunk;
you do not belong in this category.'
I indulged in intoxication,
and brimmed with exuberance.

63

It was said:
'You have not been killed;
you have not been immersed in happiness.'
In the presence of the Beloved,
I experienced complete annihilation and abandonment.

64

You were described as clever,
but also influenced by illusion and uncertainty.
I was deceived, terrified,
and completely cut off from everything.

65

It was noted that you have become both a source of light
and a central point of attention for this gathering.
But it is also observed that your effectiveness
as a source of light is only partial,
as the other half of your presence is like circling smoke.

66

He said:
'You possess the qualities of a Sheikh,
a person of leadership and guidance.'
Before this, I did not hold the title of a Sheikh.
However, following your directive,
I have now assumed the role of your servant.

67

You have such a captivating effect on a fish
that the entire sea is drawn towards you
when you are fishing.

68

I pleaded with my beloved:
'Do not harm me with your unkindness.'
She replied that a person
is like a protective outer layer,
concealing a valuable jewel within.
'The revelation of that pearl will not occur
until you experience complete brokenness,
O passionate lover.'
Does the pearl serve as an idol,
or does it merely reflect the form of my idol?

69

If you are a seed, birds will peck at you.
If you are a flower, children will pick you.
Conceal the seed completely and turn, rather, into a snare.
Hide the blossom, and become mere moss on a rooftop.

70

Inside you lies an Egypt,
and you are its realm of delightful pleasure.
Why worry if you lack outside help in obtaining sugar?

Part 8

The Place of Words
in the Path of Awareness

71

Words and names can be likened to snares or pitfalls.
Pleasant words are like grains of sand
in the flowing current of existence.

72

The Divine and Radiant Being hides itself within the
orchard, concealed in the chaos of words.
In the midst of sounds, words, and dialogue,
a veil forms that offers only the scent of the apple,
but not the fruit itself.

73

What is the definition of a word for?
So that you contemplate it.
What is the definition of a word?
An obstruction jutting out from the garden wall.

74

As the ocean has no shore,
keep your lips sealed.
This boundless sea of sweetness
knows no limits or bounds.

75

Do not view this discourse as the essence of existence; instead, seek renewed vitality within ancient vocabulary.

76

There is no expression that has not been hidden,
concealed time and again across the world.
These names and words, admired and exalted,
emerge solely from the outward manifestation of humanity.

77

Words are like nests,
while meanings resemble birds.
The physical form is like a stream,
while the essence or soul is like the flowing water.

78

My only lament, beyond the pursuit of rhyme,
was that poetry also liberated me from itself.
Deconstruct and dismantle this poetry
as you would an antiquated verse,
for interpretations transcend
mere words and the fleeting nature of air.

79

My beloved urges me to endure,
thinking beyond our moments together.
'Be content, my poetic admirer,
for rhyme becomes your advantage in my presence.'
'I will unsettle words, speech, and sound,
so that with you, I can transcend all three.'

80

Disregard the rhyme and metre,
for they are superficial
and fail to capture the true essence of poets.

Part 9

The Role of Seeking in Awareness

81

Always keep your gaze fixed on the celestial sphere
in the ethereal realm; sway gracefully like a willow.
Water and fire will constantly enhance
your nourishment from above.

82

O saviour and bestower of intellect,
one cannot desire what is not willed by You.
Both the act of seeking and the essence of goodness
stem from You.
We are insignificant:
You are the beginning and the end.

83

This phrase is delightful,
like the nourishing essence of the soul.
The soul cannot find satisfaction without an earnest seeker.
When the listener is parched and filled with anticipation,
even a silent preacher transforms into an orator.

84

This patience stems from your instruction,
as longing must be nurtured and unwavering.
A stream that perpetually flows
remains free of contamination or stagnation.

85

Escaping from a wolf is not optional,
but it is possible to flee from an unsuitable place.

86

Your sincerity led you to search,
and your search led me to your sincerity.

87

God,
alter the course of the ocean,
though those by the shore may turn pale in fear.
Yet when mercy's grace arrives,
their faces blush with the glow of the jewel.
A pallid complexion is desirable,
for it eagerly anticipates that sacred encounter.

88

No matter how quickly you search,
in the end you will discover what you seek.
It is wise to always use both hands in your pursuit,
for searching is a valuable compass on the journey.

89

Exhibit patience and perseverance
when fasting from worldly desires,
continuously awaiting provision from God.
The benevolent and tolerant deity bestows blessings
upon those who demonstrate patience.

90

The being that traverses from one ocean to another
leaves from its source
and ultimately returns to its point of origin.
The soul, infused with love,
rushes from our bodies like swift torrents
flowing from the headwaters.

Part 10
Action & Growth

91

A person's secret is like the root of a tree,
serving as the foundation
from which strong wood and
flourishing growth arise.

92

An action in the unseen realm has consequences,
and its results are beyond human control.

93

Action is a subset of perception;
a person is merely the opening of the eye.

94

If dishonesty is present in the testimony of two witnesses,
their evidence will be dismissed in the court
of Divine Justice.

95

Genuine work belongs to the person
who adheres to the principles of Truth,
dedicating themselves solely to that pursuit
and neglecting all other obligations.
Some, like children, spend their days in recreation
until the inevitable night of departure arrives.

96

Actions and speech serve as windows into your true nature: both unveil concealed mysteries.

97

He thought: Riches are within the confines of my home,
so why does destitution
and sorrow persist within these walls?
I have died in poverty despite this treasure,
as I am shrouded in ignorance and
obscured from the truth.

98

We gather wheat in this warehouse,
yet we end up losing the harvested grain.
We do not blame the defect on the cleverness of the mouse.
A mouse has snuck into our warehouse,
and through its cunning our storehouse has been ruined.

99

It is recognized that if you do not experience
sorrow or sadness,
the consequences of your actions
will eventually catch up with you.

100

By maintaining a state of vigilance and wakefulness,
you can perceive the immediate consequences
of your actions in every moment.

Finis